WHAT THE GOP
CAN LEARN FROM NIKE

Affinity Press
New York, New York

affinitypressbooks.com

Copyright 2014 © by Bill Shireman

ISBN 10: 1499364318
ISBN 13: 978-1499364316

WHAT THE GOP CAN LEARN FROM NIKE

AMERICA'S CREATIVE,
ENTREPRENEURIAL,
CAN-DO MAJORITY –

AND HOW TO WIN IT BACK

By Bill Shireman

INTRODUCTION

American support for core Republican principles – like individual freedom, personal responsibility, innovation, entrepreneurship, and self-reliance – is at an all-time high. Polls suggest that, based on support for these principles, Republicans should outnumber Democrats almost two-to-one.

But as the report "Grand Old Party for a New Generation" by the College Republican National Committee (CRNC) illustrated, the Republican brand has been badly damaged, and nearly destroyed among large blocks of voters, by a succession of campaigns during which critics have defined the party as anti-women, anti-Hispanic, anti-gay, anti-middle class, and anti-environment.

Some of the wounds were self-inflicted, from the infamous "47%" remarks made by Mitt Romney to the "legitimate rape" comments made by Rep. Todd Akin in his Senate campaign. Others were salted regularly by media and political opponents to deepen the wounds and keep them fresh. The damage was significant. "Young voters simply felt the GOP had nothing to offer, and therefore said they trusted the Democratic Party more than the Republican Party on every issue tested," CRNC found.

Just 28% to 33% of young voters said they have a positive view of the Republican Party. Over 50% had a negative view. Among "winnable" young voters – those who sided with Romney on most issues but voted for Obama anyway – the words that most often come to mind when they think of words that most often come to mind when they think of Republicans were "closed-minded, racist, rigid, (and) old-fashioned."

"It is not that young voters are enamored of the Democratic Party," according to the CRNC. "They simply dislike the Republican Party more."

That makes the GOP's battle for a national resurgence daunting, especially given that only 25% of voters identify as Republican according to a recent Gallup poll. Were the party's brand not so badly damaged, it could attract a majority of voters through modest adjustments on marriage equality, immigration, entrepreneurship, environment, and the roles of women.

Before voters can be attracted back, they first need to buy into the brand. Yet today, the party that established itself as the party of freedom and equality opportunity for all Americans is often seen as a rich white man's party. According to CRNC, "Mitt Romney won young white voters by a 7-point margin but still lost the race. It could be said that the GOP's young voter problem is as much about failing to gain support from the African American and Latino communities as anything else. With non-white voters making up 42% of voters under the age of 30, the issue of party diversity and the party's success with the youth vote are absolutely inseparable."

LOOK LEFT, LOOK RIGHT,
MOVE FORWARD

I come to this as a lifelong Republican who often advocates for the objectives of liberals, using the principles of conservatives. I've found that if I want to understand our problems, it's important to look to the left. If I want to understand our solutions, it's important to look to the right.

Of course, like we learned in school, it's best to look both ways. The right is often first to understand the importance of standing with tradition; the left is bolder at stepping into the crosswalk. The two together provide a healthy rule-of-thumb: look both ways, and then step forward.

But the GOP had better move quickly. American politics is in the beginning stages of an historic realignment – one that will transform both major parties.

The transformation could realign the parties as early as 2016, or as late as 2020. It may be triggered by a revolt among donors, or by grassroots groups. It could result in a new Republican Party, or a third party to replace it. It could turn the Democratic Party sharply to the old left, or bring it new supporters from middle America. It could unite social liberals with business-oriented conservatives, anti-corporate progressives with Tea Partiers, fiscal conservatives with social libertarians, or some combination of these.

What the realignment looks like depends in part on chance, but significantly on strategy. Shaping a realignment that serves the interests of America as a whole takes both idealism and realism. We must be idealists in what we seek, but realists in how to get there. Neither God nor nature gives credit for good intentions.

The Republican Brand
is Not its Packaging

House Majority Leader Eric Cantor has likened the GOP's brand problem to that of a pizza company, saying that the party needs to focus on changing the "pizza box" rather than the "pizza."

But as any corporate brand executive knows, a brand is a lot more than a logo and a slogan on a box. In business, a brand doesn't consist of a product's packaging, or its attributes, or even the policies of the company that offers it. The brand is much more. It represents the soul of the product, and the enterprise that stands behind it. It is what makes the product more than physical, and the company more than a profit-maximizing machine. The brand makes it human.

In today's political game, the object of play is to demonize the enemy – to sap him or her of humanity in the eyes of voters. There is nothing new in this: demonizing the enemy is tribal in its origins, and helps us eliminate emotion from our calculus in battle, so we can readily overpower those who might threaten us, with no sense of guilt.

So Democratic strategists demonize Republicans as soulless defenders of rich and powerful corporate titans, and Republican strategists demonize Democrats as soulless Communists determined to help the "dependent 47%" suck dry the prosperity earned by hard-working Americans and the job creators who hired them.

5

Today, the Democrats are winning the game of demonization, at least at the ballot box. But it hasn't always been this way.

If Republicans are to regain our brand, our humanity, then we can learn something from those whose reputations are even more vital to their survival: the nation's Top 100 brands.

> *American politics is in the beginning stages of an historic realignment – one that will transform both major parties.*

Look at the list of Top 100 brands, and you will find a set of assets that often comprise 50% or more of a company's total valuation. Take away everything the company owns or controls – its factories, offices, raw materials, products, employees, and even intellectual property – and it would still retain half its market value, simply because of this fuzzy attribute known as its brand.

Nike is a prime example. In the mid-1990s, Nike's global brand was buffeted when the company was held responsible for using child labor to stitch soccer balls.

At first, the company ignored the charges. Later, it denied its responsibility. As the controversy grew, it pointed to the exaggerations of its accusers, and to their self-interest in using the company as a fundraising tool.

Finally, it began to realize the costs of the campaign – both direct and immediate, and indirect and long-term.

The direct immediate costs were manageable. The Nike stock valuation dipped a few points. However, the indirect long-term cost posed a much greater risk. The child labor issue took a vital, living brand, and topped off its growth potential. It signaled to consumers that Nike was no longer trendy, no longer current, no longer something they automatically wanted to be associated with.

People didn't stop buying Nike shoes – they just stopped preferring them to others. The market became open to competitors who might prove themselves more current, more soulful, and better aligned with their perspectives and values.

The result was that between 1996 and 2000, Nike's share of the footwear market slid from 55% to 39%, while Adidas more than doubled, from 6% to 15%. Nike's brand lost some of its luster and currency. Consumers told pollsters they associated three qualities with the brand: "athletics," "cool," and "bad labor practices."

By following Nike's example, Republicans can learn how to restore our brand and revise our policies, without abandoning our principles.

What Nike realized is that the cost of being associated with child labor can be looked at in two ways: first, how much dollar value has been shaved off? Maybe a percent or two – equal to a few hundred million dollars. Not much, from a big picture perspective. But the other way is: how does it affect the trajectory of brand value? Does this "top off" the brand, and signal that it will now enter a period of decline, where people stop feeling so attached to it, and begin to let go? Is this the issue that dehumanizes the brand, and makes it a non-living remnant of the past generation, rather than the next generation?

They realized they had to appeal to that next generation – that the erosion of the brand can be best understood not as a loss of money, but as a loss of currency, and of humanity.

People might have still liked Nike shoes just about as much as they always did. But they saw the company that made the shoes as something less human, and more machinelike; less tomorrow, or more yesterday; less living, and more dying, or dead.

That's where the Republican Party finds itself. On core principles, it is aligned with most young people, Hispanics, and women. On policies, it faces a significant gap, but one it can close. But on soul, the Republican Party is far, far away. It signals at every turn that it is a party of yesterday, not tomorrow; of the dying, not the newly born.

Of course, the Democratic Party is not far behind. But its dilemma is reversed. On policies, it is old school, 1960s vintage. On principles, it is also out-of-date, locked into a manufacturing-era mindset where workers are well-paid dependents of big corporations and big government. But where it counts, on soul, on humanity, on currency, it is a member of the family. It seems to genuinely care about young people, women, blacks, and Hispanics. It seems to have their best interests at heart, even if it's not too successful in advancing them. At least it is trying.

Stand on Principle.
Embrace Diversity.
Restore Humanity

There is a tendency on the left to equate "equality" with "sameness." This brings two negative consequences: prejudice and conformity.

Prejudice results when we treat whole populations as if every member were exactly the same – all women, all men, all blacks, all Hispanics, and so on. That invites sweeping assertions about the nature of these human classifications, encouraging people to treat an entire class as strong or weak, oppressed or oppressive.

Conformity results when we pretend that diversity is simply a matter of surface-level physical characteristics. Some define "diversity" as a condition where all people look different but think the same.

Genuine diversity is much richer in its forms. Republicans should champion diversity in its truer sense. People are different. No two of us are alike. These differences draw us together and make us stronger and more whole. Treating us as if we were no different from anyone else in our ethnic, racial, or gender "class" discounts everything about us that is unique. It weakens us all because it denies us the chance to contribute that which we uniquely bring.

Republicans champion the qualities that our collective selves bring to the whole – the contributions of women, men, blacks, Hispanics, and others. But we value even more the infinitely more varied qualities that distinct human beings bring. We seek to unleash the power and purpose that lies latent within every individual. This is the kind of melting pot in which every distinct taste is retained, yet comes together with every other to create an extraordinary whole. America's diversity draws us together and unites us.

The Democratic Party's advantage comes through by contrast to the GOP: it's not that the Democratic Party seems fully soulful and human. It's just that it seems more so, by comparison. Where Rush Limbaugh and Fox News are angry and denigrating, Jon Stewart and Stephen Colbert are fun and able to both give and take a joke.

Young voters want three qualities in their candidates: intelligence, hard work, and responsibility. Voters don't believe Republican candidates have those qualities.

By following Nike's example, Republicans can learn how to restore our brand and revise our policies, without abandoning our principles. Nike turned itself around. First, they stemmed the blood flow, by acknowledging that child labor was a problem, and accepting some of the responsibility. Virtually overnight, they became the biggest driver for the elimination of child labor, not just by reputation, but also through results.

But they also began a broad rebranding effort, aimed at re-establishing their reputation as a company that was human, and honestly cared, a lot, about the people who they wanted to buy their products.

Nike embraced women – they became advocates for the idea that women are powerful, even pressing the edges a bit, irritating established interests. They embraced ethnic minorities and the emerging new multi-ethnic majority. They embraced young people. They embraced the environment, leading other companies both on performance and policy.

> *It is essential for Republicans to have a 21st century plan that can grow the economy through innovation, not unregulated drilling or unrestrained spending.*

They didn't stop making shoes. They didn't change their commitment to quality. They didn't throw away their existing humanity, what they stood for: quality athletic gear that empowers each individual to "just do it."

Most relevant, they broadened their appeal, championing many of the same values that the Republican Party does: personal responsibility; individual discipline; exercising the power already vested within every person. They didn't adopt a "liberal" agenda that people are victims, that they have no personal power, that they need to be supported with comfy chairs, that they have to coalesce together in an alliance of the powerless to take money from the powerful. They celebrated the power in every individual; the self-discipline and enlightenment it takes to discover and harness that power.

Today, Nike is a company more associated with Democrats than with Republicans. Why? Because they reflect the soul of the Republican Party more than the party itself seems to. With help from the Democrats and, occasionally, its own candidates, the GOP is easy to position as anti-women, anti-minority, anti-youth, anti-change, anti-planet, and anti-future.

This is not new news: the party is trapped. The base is dominated by true-believers who, like all ideologues, believe their righteousness is so self-evident that a majority will bend to their will, if they just stay rigid and inflexible.

Some reflexively broad-brush all gay, feminist, and Hispanic leaders as their enemies, even though many believe just as fervently in personal freedom and responsibility, and refuse to think of themselves as victims. Those are small "r" republicans – but the idea of joining the party is big "r" Repugnant to many of them.

These are precisely the people the party could appeal to, if it weren't dragged down by its brand. These people reject the idea that they need government to decide with whom they sleep, what nation they live in, and what they should do with their lives. They are people who

know they don't live in the coal age, they don't need to choose between prosperity and the environment, and they don't have to live the same lifestyle that Tom Brokaw's "Greatest Generation" did.

At every turn, these could-be Republicans hear that they don't belong in the Republican Party.

YES:

Intelligent, Hard Working, and Responsible

NO:

Irresponsible, Incompetent, and Closed-Minded

Young voters want three qualities in their candidates: intelligence, hard work, and responsibility. "Intelligent … emerged as the most sought-after quality in a candidate, chosen by 34%, followed by 'hardworking' and 'responsible' at 28% each. They were then followed by 'open-minded' and 'principled' at 26%, and 'competent' at 24%."

But by a wide margin, voters don't believe Republican candidates have those qualities. Only 14% said they are intelligent, just 18% said hard-working, and 17% said entrepreneurial.

The most disliked qualities for a candidate were "irresponsible" and "incompetent," tied at 32%, followed closely by "closed-minded" at 29% - qualities they often associated with Republican candidates.

For the GOP to attract young people across all categories, it must once again value intelligence first. When it comes to these voters, the CRNC reported, "If the GOP is thought of as the 'stupid party,' it may as well be the kiss of death."

A Party for the Rich – Not for Families?

Ronald Reagan once said, "Latinos are Republicans – they just don't know it yet." Well, many Republicans apparently don't know it either. The CRNC focus groups revealed a common impression of the party by Hispanic voters. As one woman said, "Focusing on the Mexican culture and how they view Republicans, the Mexican culture tends to be more a family-oriented, warm, home – attention to others, help your neighbors, you cook them a meal if you know that they're struggling."

She continued: "Republicans are more like, yeah, I'll scratch your back only if you are my neighbor here in the high society, or whatever." The GOP, she suggested, is not her brand. Its people are rich cronies.

The Party That
Couldn't Even Try

An August 2012 survey showed that Obama's standing had fallen sharply from four years prior, and that young people were not strongly in favor of all of his policies. Just 20% thought the economy had gotten better in the last year, and 22% thought Obama's policies had made it easier for young people to get a job. Only 29% thought the stimulus package had benefited them.

Yet despite their failings, Democrats held a 16-point advantage over the Republican Party among young voters on handling of the economy and jobs. Among the respondents who said they approved of the job Obama had been doing, the number one word they used was "Trying." He was trying. As CRNC said, "Young voters were disappointed in Obama's performance, but gave him credit for attempting to improve the situation. In our focus groups, many respondents strongly defended President Obama even while acknowledging the mediocrity of the last four years."

Toward a Renewed
Republican Brand

The CRNC had good news for the GOP as well. "On many of the issues that matter most to young people, there is a clear path forward for Republican candidates, and with messaging that explains what we are for and not just what we are against, we can begin to rebuild standing with young people on key policy issues."

Here are eight ways the GOP can learn both from Nike's experience, and from the values conveyed by its brand.

1. Innovation – Not Stimulus – Drives Economic Growth
2. Freedom and Responsibility, Not Dependence, Lead to Prosperity
3. Microenterprise and Entrepreneurism Drive Innovation
4. Overtaxing Small Business Hurts the Economy
5. Economic Growth or the Environment? Both!
6. Women, Power, and Choice
7. Hispanics, Immigration, and Cultural Integration: Make it Easier to Do It the Right Way
8. Value Families in Many Forms

1

INNOVATION – NOT STIMULUS – DRIVES ECONOMIC GROWTH

Republicans have an opportunity to capture young peoples' imagination with a 21st century vision of prosperity, one founded not on big government spending, but on the kind of innovation they have learned to expect from a free market economy.

Yet when many Republicans talk about growing the economy, they still emphasize the need to "drill-baby-drill," to achieve "energy independence" – something they have been trying to do since President Nixon's term. That traps them in a narrative that pits the economy against the environment. Before long, their economic growth plan is to strip the "job-killing EPA" of its regulatory power, so big companies can extract more oil faster.

Of course, EPA regulations can and do kill jobs, which is one reason why only 20% of young people in the Spring 2012 Harvard Institute of Politics survey believe that "government spending is an effective way to increase economic growth." But focusing first on EPA strikes the young as out of touch. They know regulations can kill jobs – but they also know poor safety practices can kill people. The anti-regulatory message cuts both ways for them.

The GOP can't win by opposing all regulations. It needs to acknowledge that some regulations are needed, while showing how easily most can be hijacked to support vested interests rather than their public purpose. The party must favor safety and responsibility; its critique of regulations must flow from this purpose.

Young voters also know we need energy to thrive. Some 51% of young voters think they would be at least somewhat better off if more oil and natural gas exploration was permitted. But they know better than some party leaders that fossil fuels are just one of the ingredients. Much more important is the human component: our ability to create value.

It is essential for Republicans to have a 21st century plan to grow prosperity through innovation, not unregulated drilling or unrestrained spending, and enable young people to make choices about family and home on their own terms, without putting them off due to a poor economy.

2

FREEDOM AND RESPONSIBILITY,
NOT DEPENDENCY,
LEAD TO PROSPERITY

Young voters, empowered by technologies that give them more choices than their parents, are fiercely dedicated to personal freedom, entrepreneurship, and finding their own path. They don't look to corporations or government as sources of lifetime support, but only as way stations that they can tap as needed, and for a price.

Growing up during decades of cultural dynamism and political gridlock, young voters favor free enterprise but distrust both government and corporate power, and the more job experience they have, the less dependent on government they feel. Some 51% of those aged 18 to 24 and 64% of those 25-to-32 prefer "smaller government with fewer services but lower taxes," according to a poll conducted in Summer of 2013 by inc./WomanTrend for FreedomWorks.

Three-quarters of the 18-to-32-year-olds said they believe current economic conditions can be changed by the federal government in Washington. But most feel that, during their lifetimes, the changes brought by Washington have been for the worse. Two-thirds believe their generation will be worse off than their parents'. Many are delaying buying a home, saving for retirement, starting a family and getting married because of the economy.

Young voters know there is a role for both corporations and government. But they don't trust either. They distrust the motives of corporations, and the competence of government.

On Social Security, Medicare, student loans and other middle class government subsidies, young voters know that, either through government mismanagement or corporate self-interest, the programs are headed for disaster. Fully 90% of respondents agree with the statement, "We need to reform Social Security and Medicare now so that the next generation isn't left cleaning up a huge mess down the road." Some 58% say they would be better off if Medicare and Medicaid were reformed so they cost less in the future.

On student loans, CRNC suggests that "Republicans should offer a way forward that doesn't just propose to subsidize the problem of sky-high tuition; they should offer solutions that would help make an education more affordable in the first place. In Texas, Gov. Rick Perry has issued a challenge to institutions to create the "$10,000 bachelor's degree," and in Indiana, then-Gov. Mitch Daniels helped establish Western Governors University Indiana, a non-profit, competency based university developed by a bipartisan group of governors and education innovators.

An innovation agenda for higher education would do much more for the young than driving costs higher with even more cheap student loan money.

3

MICROENTERPRISE AND ENTREPRENEURISM DRIVE INNOVATION

The CRNC found that "young people are incredibly eager to be entrepreneurs and to start their own businesses. Some 45% in the August 2012 XG study, including 58% of black and 64% of Hispanic respondents, said they hoped to start their own business one day. As one participant in a focus group of young aspiring entrepreneurs in Orlando, FL put it: 'We should really try to find out, what barriers do people have towards being successful and of being hardworking, educating themselves, and trying to improve the economy and so on, and work on maybe reducing the obstacles there.'"

Yet the GOP consistently fumbles opportunities to highlight its support of today's entrepreneurism. During October of the 2012 campaign, the Romney campaign declined an offer by MTV to interview both presidential candidates on air. President Obama agreed, and was asked to address the concerns of young people who aspire to be the "next Mark Zuckerberg" by explaining what he would do to make it easier for young people to start their own business. "The president's response was masterful," CRNC reported. "He remarked on how he had worked to remove financial regulations that prohibited small investors from contributing money online, unleashing the ability of crowdfunding sites like Kickstarter to help young entrepreneurs raise capital. The legislation Obama is referring to in this response is the JOBS, or Jump Start Our Business Startups Act, a bill passed in Congress with wide bipartisan support including the vocal backing of Republican House Majority Leader Eric Cantor. It offered the perfect example of a policy targeted at enabling entrepreneurship, removing barriers to opportunity, and actually repealing harmful, stifling government regulation. Best yet, it was something positive – something to stand for rather than simply an Obama policy to stand against. It is examples like this of policies that align perfectly with conservative principles, that actually pull back the obstacles created by government and unleash the power of small business, that must be at the heart of an economic agenda that can appeal to young voters."

4

OVERTAXING SMALL BUSINESS HURTS THE ECONOMY

Most prospective Republican voters don't believe cutting corporate tax rates will help them. "Only 34% … thought they'd be better off if the corporate tax rate were lowered, and only 36% thought such a move would make it easier for young people to get jobs. Only 40% thought they'd be better off if regulations on business were reduced.

"Yet change the phrasing to emphasize small business and a completely different picture emerges. Some 67% of young people in that survey said that 'keeping taxes low on small businesses' would make it easier for young people to get jobs. Some 49% thought that 'reducing regulations on small businesses' would make it easier for young people to get jobs."

In focus groups of young aspiring entrepreneurs who voted for Obama, "respondents noted that Republicans were the more 'pro-business' party. Yet when asked why they voted Democratic despite their desire to start a business themselves, the responses were clear: 'I don't think [the Republicans] would make it easier for small businesses.' 'A corporation, maybe, absolutely. A small business?' 'The Republican Party would make it really easy to start a business and have a successful business if you already have that capital in your bank account, because you're not losing that money. But we're all sitting on our own various debts and our student loans, and the Republican Party isn't helping us with any of that.'"

To win these voters, the GOP needs to articulate an innovation agenda that genuinely drives entrepreneurship and transparently supports enterprises of all size.

5

ECONOMIC GROWTH
OR THE ENVIRONMENT?

BOTH!

Young voters reject the idea that to grow the economy you have to damage the environment. This is not the coal age. This is three generations into the information economy. Environmental protection is fully compatible with economic growth. It's expected – it's assumed.

When forced to choose, young voters split about evenly, giving a slight edge to the environment. A March 2013 Gallup survey of American adults showed more 18 to 29 year-olds saying environmental protection should take priority (49%) than those saying economic growth should take priority (45%).

Yet in terms of urgency, the economy needs help right now. People need jobs to put food on the table today. They need the environment to live for the long term. So 45% want political leaders focused on the economy as their top priority, while only 8% want them focused first on climate change, according to CRNC.

Republican climate "skeptics" use that data to argue that young voters don't care much about the environment. Yet a majority of young conservatives under age 35 – 30% of whom doubt climate change is real – still favor action on climate.

Here's where young voters differ with the Democratic Party on the issue: they are "not all convinced that government action on issues like climate change and green energy would be positive overall."

Nonetheless, if nothing else is on the table, they favor government action. About 80% of voters under age 35 support "President Obama's climate change plan" – even though most have no idea what's in that plan. But they favor action. If the GOP doesn't offer an action plan, they won't expend a lot of effort to figure out a better approach – they will take what's on the table that the Democrats set.

The failure of the GOP to offer a climate policy of its own makes a big government approach a self-fulfilling prophecy.

Messages that assume the economy and environment are at odds are counterproductive, and damage the Republican brand. Focusing on the "job-killing EPA" may be valid, but also sends two wrong messages: first, that Republicans will sacrifice the environment to benefit a special interest group, and second that they hold the view that to grow the economy, they have to sacrifice the environment and benefit a special interest. This makes them look old and out of touch.

The failure of the GOP to offer a climate policy of its own makes a big government approach a self-fulfilling prophecy. GOP leaders rightly worry that a Democrat-led climate policy will lead to more regulations, higher costs, and higher taxes. Rather than offering no alternative, strategic Republicans could seize the high ground on the issue.

For example, former Secretary of State George Shultz has proposed a "Climate Insurance Policy" approach that emulates the GOP's leadership on ozone protection during the Reagan administration. "There were ozone skeptics back then, just as there are climate skeptics now," Shultz said. "But we all agreed that, if what some scientists feared were to happen, it would be disastrous. So we agreed to take out an insurance policy." The Montreal Protocol quickly led to innovations that vastly reduced ozone depleting substances. "In retrospect, the non-skeptics turned out to be right, and the Montreal Protocol came around just in time."

80% of voters under age 35 support "President Obama's climate change plan" – even though most have no idea what's in that plan.

On climate, Shultz's policy preference combines sound policy with deft strategy. It would lead to long-term tax and spending reductions, by shifting taxes from forms of prosperity that tend to go up (income, profits, savings, and payroll) to forms of pollution we seek to drive down (carbon and other pollutants). While the initial tax cut would be small, in the long term taxes would decline significantly.

Greg Mankiw, Arthur Laffer, Luigi Zingales and many other conservative economists have proposed a federal "carbon tax shift" that would cut taxes on income or payroll, and make up the difference with a price on carbon. Consumer product companies and retailers have noted that it puts more money in the pockets of "WalMart moms." ExxonMobil CEO Rex Tillerson has endorsed the proposal as a rational approach to climate risk. Economically, the shift would increase jobs, income, technology and innovation – the things young voters desire. It would smooth the transition toward natural gas and away from coal, while delivering most of its tax benefits to coal states.

Carbon, unfortunately, has become an ideological litmus test on both the left and right. The hard left uses it to drive home the need for economy-wide regulation. The hard right resists it just as strenuously, to avoid such regulation. Republicans may be more successful if they support a pollution tax shift that covers a "market basket" of contaminants, rather than just carbon, as an alternative to onerous EPA carbon mandates. Pollution taxes are the one form of taxation that a plurality of GOP voters actually supports, according to polls by Hart Research.

Even if some GOP lawmakers remained skeptical, the party would seize the issue from Democrats, and regain its historical conservation leadership. "All of the most important federal environmental actions were taken by Republican presidents," Shultz reminds us.

Nike didn't demand that customers accept worker exploitation as a precondition for getting their shoes. They delivered the shoes first — but they promised, and their customers expected, that they would learn how to do it without hurting workers or the environment.

If the Republican Party can't do the same on the economy, maybe it doesn't need to be in business much longer. People can get their shoes elsewhere.

6

WOMEN, POWER, AND CHOICE

Women often achieve leadership positions on the right. Margaret Thatcher is venerated. Condoleeza Rice was a sensible source of counsel in an administration of firebrands. Sarah Palin was held in high esteem by many. Anne Coulter, though outlandish in her rhetoric, is often revered. Michelle Bachman embodies a personal form of compassionate conservatism that few in either party could match.

By and large, Republicans have great respect for women. They regard them as strong and forceful advocates. Republicans may differ on social roles, and some view feminism harshly. But most Republicans object to the left's victimization of women – the tendency to characterize all women as oppressed. Women are smart and powerful, from the perspective of Republicans. Yes, women face genuine discrimination. But they are not without power. Quite the opposite: In the U.S., there are now more new women entrepreneurs than men. Women are better educated, their incomes are rising faster, and they are the family CFOs who direct 73% of our dollars.

Women will not stand for another generation in which the norm is to discount their salaries, careers, or power. They do not need to be given generations to heal as a class from their wounds. They are rising to take their place, now.

The GOP champions the power of women, and the combination of individual resolve and group cohesiveness that is changing America for the better. Yet the party remains extremely vulnerable to charges that it is anti-woman, and this weakness contributed greatly to its defeat in 2012.

The GOP needs to champion the elimination of barriers to women's entrepreneurship. It needs to lead the way in assuring access to capital, training, and partnership – not to women as a class, but to small entrepreneurs, most of who are now women. The party can collaborate with the large and well-established network of women's oriented businesses and organizations that are already well advanced down this path. It can align with the burgeoning population of "sharing economy" entrepreneurs starting local companies in competition with hotels, taxis, and large-scale merchants and manufacturers. The party needs to become a genuine ally to this movement, setting forth changes in decades-old local, state, and federal policies that penalize small business and favor entrenched interests, so that women recognize the party as a partner that shares their aspirations, respects their capabilities, supports their entrepreneurship, and earns their mutual trust and support.

7

HISPANICS, IMMIGRATION, AND CULTURAL INTEGRATION:

MAKE IT EASIER TO DO IT THE RIGHT WAY

Republicans and many Democrats still hold on to a "melting pot" view of American democracy, where immigrants quickly assimilate into the dominant culture and become "Americans." They are concerned that many Hispanics are not assimilating in this way – that they are establishing separate Spanish-speaking communities where they can continue to live the way they did in their birth nation, while taking advantage of the benefits of democratic free markets.

Democrats can leverage this fear, positioning the Republican Party as those who will only accept Hispanics if they erase any trace of their ethnic heritage. This creates a perverse strategic incentive to keep Spanish speakers separate from English speakers, so they remain a more solid voting block, offering support to the left more than the right.

Republicans can highlight illegal immigration, winning over Americans who fear their "native" culture will be overrun and, to some degree, displaced by invaders from the south. Democrats can leverage the Hispanophobia, and use it to position itself as the party that celebrates the contributions of Hispanics, and treats "illegals" with compassion.

Back once again in the real world, most Americans of all ages value ethnic diversity, but are concerned about separatism. They believe the many Hispanic cultural influences can be integrated into American culture, and become an organic part of it, just as others have in generations past. They need not fall for the wedge tactic of either codifying or banning the Spanish language; they can add elements of it to the composite language we first adopted, and then corrupted, from England.

How should Republicans approach illegal immigration? They know they should avoid exploiting it, even to activate the base. Doing so will stigmatize Hispanics, especially once the examples are taken up by the media. As the CRNC focus groups found, "some raised the Arizona law as an example of something they felt allowed unfair targeting of legal immigrants, and as something that made them feel less positive about the Republican Party. When asked if they thought any Republican policies were making them personally worse off, one (Hispanic) replied, 'Arizona comes to mind, all the laws that they've passed there regarding immigration and being allowed to pull somebody over just based on how they look.'"

It is also important for the Republican Party "to be clear about the difference between legal and illegal immigrants, and to also differentiate illegal immigrants from the children of illegal immigrants and how they would be affected by policies," says CRNC.

The best approach to immigration may actually be to just fix the system: streamline and simplify the process of legal immigration, and open that process to would-be Americans both inside and outside our borders. Stem the flow of immigrants through Mexico, which is increasingly not a source but a transit byway for those emigrating from further south. Sensible solutions make good political sense, especially when only 3% of young voters named immigration as their top priority issue, and only 11% in the March 2013 CRNC survey named "reforming our nation's immigration system" as one of their top two or three priorities. That approach would meet the core objectives of the two largest opinion blocks on the issue – the just-over-half of young voters who favor a path to legal status for illegal immigrants, and the just-under-half who focus on enforcement, border security, and deportation.

8

VALUE FAMILIES IN MANY FORMS

Young voters are committed to the institution of marriage, and don't believe it should be reserved for straight couples. They are also aware that the current economy makes it hard for them to start families, CRNC found. "I've been dating my girlfriend for almost five years now, and we're still not even really thinking about getting married because ...financially we're in a bad spot, as a whole generation," one of the young entrepreneurs in their Orlando focus group told them.

To young voters who might otherwise be attracted to Republican principles, "opposition to same-sex marriage constituted a 'deal breaker,'" according to CRNC. "Among those respondents who said that same-sex marriage should be legal (a full 44% of young voters), half said that they would probably or definitely not vote for a candidate with whom they disagreed on same-sex marriage, even if they were in agreement on taxes, defense, immigration, and spending."

Can the GOP win on issues of greater issue salience, so that gay marriage is not a "deal breaker" for a large number of young voters? Probably not. To these voters, marriage equality is more than a position on an issue. It is a matter of ethics and integrity. They would not support a party with so deep a character flaw, even if its surface positions were compatible.

The party's second option is to strike a middle ground. CRNC, for example, suggests that the party push a "states rights" approach, leaving issues of marriage up to candidates at the local level. That, however, is likely to backfire in short order, much more quickly than did the Democrats' alliance with segregationists in the 1960s.

I come from San Francisco, and in The City, the most determined and outspoken proponents of genuine family values are gay and lesbian couples. They know the importance of a strong two-parent family with a masculine and feminine influence, no matter the gender of the parents; a family that sacrifices for the children and never regrets it.

Why are they mostly Democrats, and not Republicans? Because they think the Republican Party rejects their qualifications for parenthood, and their capacity to live for their family, for their children.

It is important for the GOP to be on the side of history on this issue. While the party may remain divided for a few years on exactly how gay and lesbian Americans secure an equal right to form families – whether via civil unions or marriage rights – the party needs to champion these rights. The just position, and the politically expedient one, is the same: support for same sex marriage should be encouraged; eventually it will become the norm.

The Republican Party needs to follow the example of Nike. First, we need to stem the blood flow, by better conveying what unregistered Republicans want to know we understand: women, blacks, and Hispanics are and ought to be powerful. Climate change is used by Democrats and Republicans, cynically, to advance their own unrelated agendas – but the risk is real, and demands a serious response. Prosperity is our most urgent need, and achieving it does not mean sacrificing the environment. Family values have some of their most powerful advocates in those just given the right to be a family. American ideals are often most vigorously championed by those who have fought for the right to be Americans, whether on the battlefield, in the immigration process, or risking their lives to cross into our nation in order to be free and the GOP needs to include these individuals if it hopes to survive.

ABOUT THE AUTHOR

Future 500 CEO Bill Shireman places himself between groups that love to hate and demonize each other: the right and left, Rush Limbaugh conservatives and Michael Moore progressives, and above all, the world's best-known companies and most impassioned activist groups. Called a "master social and environmental entrepreneur," Shireman has successfully united business and civic leaders behind systems-based solutions that actually work, to clean up the environment, recycle resources, promote human rights, and help solve some of the world's most challenging problems. He believes those solutions can be found in the principles that underlie the two most innovative systems on the planet: the rainforest and the economy – free-flowing markets and free-flowing ecosystems. These systems are more complex than any ideology, yet they operate according to simple and powerful principles, like feedback, adaptation, and continuous innovation. He fails all political litmus tests, seeking instead to understand the elements of truth in all belief systems, how to combine them to form higher truths, and how to apply them in the real world to solve real problems.

* * *

The views expressed here are those of the author, to help stimulate fresh thinking about the future of the Republican Party. The opinions do not reflect those of Future 500 or any of our stakeholders, and are subject to change upon receipt of better information or convincing argument.

www.ingramcontent.com/pod-product-compliance
Lightning Source LLC
Chambersburg PA
CBHW021209290526
45796CB00006B/38